The Wreck on the 5:25

by Thornton Wilder

A Samuel French Acting Edition

SAMUELFRENCH.COM

Copyright © 1957, 1961
Yale University, Fisk University and Oberlin College
Foreword copyright © 2014 by Tappan Wilder
All Rights Reserved

THE WRECK ON THE 5:25 is fully protected under the copyright laws of the United States of America and all countries with which the United States has reciprocal copyright relations, whether through bilateral or multi-lateral treaties or otherwise, and including but not limited to, all countries covered by the Pan-American Copyright Convention, the Universal Copyright Convention, and the Berne Convention. All rights, including professional and amateur stage productions, recitation, lecturing, public reading, motion picture, radio broadcasting, television and the rights of translation into foreign languages are strictly reserved.

ISBN 978-0-573-70390-4

www.SamuelFrench.com
www.SamuelFrench-London.co.uk

For Production Enquiries

United States and Canada
Info@SamuelFrench.com
1-866-598-8449

Amateur Rights in the United Kingdom
Plays@SamuelFrench-London.co.uk
020-7255-4302

Each title is subject to availability from Samuel French, depending upon country of performance. Please be aware that *THE WRECK ON THE 5:25* may not be licensed by Samuel French in your territory. Producers should contact the nearest Samuel French office or licensing partner to verify availability.

For all enquiries regarding Professional productions in the United Kingdom; Professional and Amateur productions throughout the rest of Europe; and motion picture, television, and other media rights, please contact Alan Brodie Representation (Victoria@AlanBrodie.com). Visit www.thorntonwilder.com/contact for details.

CAUTION: Professional and amateur producers are hereby warned that *THE WRECK ON THE 5:25* is subject to a licensing fee. Publication of this play does not imply availability for performance. Professionals and Amateurs considering a production are strongly advised to apply for a license before starting rehearsals, advertising, or booking a theatre. A licensing fee must be paid whether the title is presented for charity or gain and whether or not admission is charged.

No one shall make any changes in this title for the purpose of production. No part of this book may be reproduced, stored in a retrieval system, or transmitted in any form, by any means, now known or yet to be invented, including mechanical, electronic, photocopying, recording, videotaping, or otherwise, without the prior written permission of the publisher. No one shall upload this title, or part of this title, to any social media websites.

MUSIC USE NOTE

Licensees are solely responsible for obtaining formal written permission from copyright owners to use copyrighted music in the performance of this play and are strongly cautioned to do so. If no such permission is obtained by the licensee, then the licensee must use only original music that the licensee owns and controls. Licensees are solely responsible and liable for all music clearances and shall indemnify the copyright owners of the play and their licensing agent, Samuel French, against any costs, expenses, losses and liabilities arising from the use of music by licensees. Please contact the appropriate music licensing authority in your territory for the rights to any incidental music.

IMPORTANT BILLING AND CREDIT REQUIREMENTS

All producers of *THE WRECK ON THE 5:25* must give credit to the author of the play in all programs distributed in connection with performances of the play, and in all instances in which the title of the play appears for the purposes of advertising, publicizing or otherwise exploiting the play and/or a production. The name of the author must appear on a separate line on which no other name appears, immediately following the title and must appear in size of type not less than fifty percent of the size of the title type.

This play may be performed only in its entirety. No permission can be granted for cuttings, readings or any use of parts of the play for any purpose whatsoever without the express written permission of the Wilder Family LLC. Absolutely *no* changes can be made to the text.

FOREWORD TO WILDER'S
THE WRECK ON THE 5:25

THE SIN OF SLOTH

From the time he began dreaming up plays as a boy Thornton Wilder's vision of the theater transcended conventional boundaries, and to the end of his life his vision continually evolved and expanded. In 1956, he began work on what grew into an extravagantly ambitious project: two cycles of seven one-act plays based on the Deadly Sins and the Ages of Man. *The Wreck on the 2:25* represents "Sloth" in Wilder's projected cycle on the Seven Deadly Sins.

In what would prove to be his final dramatic works, Wilder sought not only to explore the theatrical possibilities inherent in the Sins and Ages, but (as he phrased it in his private journal on Christmas Day 1960) to "offer each play in the series as representing, also, a different mode of playwriting: Grand Guignol, Chekhov, Noh play, etc., etc." In short, he envisioned nothing less than a *tour de force* of dramatic theme and form encapsulated in the economy and intensity of the one-act play.

Wilder did not complete the challenge he set for himself, but he came close. The surviving work enriches his dramatic legacy and deserves to be remembered as more than a footnote to his lifelong conviction (written soon after *Our Town* opened on Broadway in 1938): "The theater offers to imaginative narration its highest possibilities."

THE SINS AND AGES THEN AND NOW

A brief overview of the history of these plays will help readers place them in Wilder's career as a dramatist. Two Sins, *Bernice* (Pride) and *The Wreck on the 5:25* (Sloth), premiered in English at a special event in Berlin in 1957 (with Wilder performing in *Bernice*). For reasons that have never been clear, for he enjoyed the experience and felt that plays did well, he withdrew them. That same year a third Sin, *The Drunken Sisters* (Gluttony), written as the satyr play for Wilder's full length drama, *The Alcestiad*, proved successful in its premiere on the stage of Zürich's fabled Schauspielhaus.

Five years passed before the continuation of his ambitious scheme appeared on a stage in the United States. In January 1962, two new Ages (*Infancy* and *Childhood*) and a new Sin, *Someone From Assisi* (Lust), opened at Circle in the Square, then located off-Broadway on Bleecker Street, to the reported largest pre-opening advanced sale in that stage's then 11-year history. Billed as "Plays for Bleecker Street," the show of ran for 349 performances.

Then silence. After "Plays for Bleecker Street" closed, no more Sins or Ages appeared. When Thornton Wilder died in 1975 the public record of his 14-play scheme contained only four plays – two Ages (*Infancy* and *Childhood*) and two Sins (Lust and Gluttony).

Today, eleven of Wilder's Sins and Ages are available for production: a completed cycle of the seven Deadly Sins and four of seven Ages of Man. The source of the seven "new" plays is no secret. The missing pieces were found in Thornton Wilder's archives at Yale[1]. From this source, starting in 1995, his literary executor and family released the two plays withdrawn in 1957, *Cement Hands* (Avarice), and four additional titles (*Youth, The Rivers Under the Earth* [Middle Age][2], *A Ringing of Doorbells* [Envy] and *In Shakespeare and the Bible* [Wrath]) recovered and completed by the actor, director and friend of Wilder's, F.J. O'Neil. (Mr. O'Neil's valuable notes on the origin of each of these missing links follow the text of each play.)

The public reception of Thornton Wilder's long lost and new plays was gratifying. *The Wreck on the 5:25* was selected as one of the Best American Short Plays of 1994-95. In 1997, the Centenary of the playwright's birth, Kevin Kline starred in a premiere reading in New York of *Cement Hands*, and the works recovered by Mr. O'Neil served as the centerpieces of Actors Theatre of Louisville's 13th Annual Brown-Forman Classics in Context Festival. Finally, as the capstone to the Centenary celebration, TCG Press in 1997 published the 11 Sins and Ages in Volume I of *The Collected Short Plays of Thornton Wilder*.

---

[1] No additional one-acts remain to be discovered in Thornton Wilder's archives at Yale.

[2] We believe Wilder intended *The Rivers Under the Earth* to represent Middle Age.

Wilder never followed conventional theatrical practice. As a young writer in his "Classic One Act Plays" of 1931, he swept away scenery and played provocative games with time and place. In the Sins and Ages, his farewell as a playwright, he is no less adventurous by way of settings, techniques, stage-craft and themes. One artistic trend of the day especially "fired his imagination" where these plays are concerned: his passionate belief in the value of the arena stage. "The boxed set play," he wrote in 1961, "encourages the anecdote…The unencumbered stage encourages the truth in everyone." Wilder felt so strongly that audiences should be seated as close to the actors as possible that Samuel French, for several years, was only permitted to license these plays to companies agreeing to perform them on a three-sided thrust or arena stage.

***

As part of its celebration of Wilder's one-act plays, Samuel French and the Wilder family take great pleasure in issuing new acting editions for the Sins and Ages long in print and, for the first time, acting editions of the seven new Wilder works. We invite those performing or teaching these plays to visit www.thorntonwilder.com for additional information.

– *Tappan Wilder,*
Literary Executor for Thornton Wilder

CHARACTERS

MRS. HAWKINS, forty
MINNIE, her daughter, almost sixteen
MR. FORBES, a neighbor
MR. HERBERT HAWKINS, Mrs. Hawkins's husband

SETTING

Today. The Hawkins home.

(Six o'clock in the evening. **MRS. HAWKINS,** *forty, and her daughter* **MINNIE,** *almost sixteen, are sewing and knitting. At the back is a door into the hall and beside it a table on which is a telephone.)*

MRS. HAWKINS. Irish stew doesn't seem right for Sunday dinner, somehow. *(pause)* And your father doesn't really like roast or veal. *(pause)* Thank Heaven, he's not crazy about steak. *(another pause while she takes some pins from her mouth)* I must say it's downright strange – his not being here. He hasn't telephoned for years, like that – that he'd take a later train.

MINNIE. Did he say what was keeping him?

MRS. HAWKINS. No…something at the office, I suppose. *(She changes pins again.)* He never really did like chicken, either.

MINNIE. He ate pork last week without saying anything. You might try pork chops, Mama; I don't really mind them.

MRS. HAWKINS. He doesn't ever say anything. He eats what's there. – Oh, Minnie, men never realize that there's only a limited number of things to eat.

MINNIE. What did he say on the telephone exactly?

MRS. HAWKINS. "I'll try to catch the six-thirty."

(Both look at their wristwatches.)

MINNIE. But, Mama, Papa's not cranky about what he eats. He's always saying what a good cook you are.

MRS. HAWKINS. Men! *(She has put down her sewing and is gazing before her.)* They think they want a lot of change – variety and change, variety and change. But they don't really. Deep down, they don't.

MINNIE. Don't what?

MRS. HAWKINS. You know for a while he read all those wild Western magazines: cowboys and horses and silly Indians...two or three a week. Then, suddenly, he stopped all that. It's as though he thought he were in a kind of jail or prison. – Keep an eye on that window, Minnie. He may be coming down the street any minute.

(**MINNIE** *rises and, turning, peers through a window, back right.*)

MINNIE. No. – There's Mr. Wilkerson, though. He came back on the five-twenty-five, anyway. Sometimes Papa stops at the tobacco shop and comes down Spruce Street.

(*She moves to the left and looks through another window.*)

MRS. HAWKINS. Do you feel as though you were in a jail, Minnie?

MINNIE. What?!

MRS. HAWKINS. As though life were a jail?

MINNIE. (*returning to her chair*) No, of course not. – Mama, you're talking awfully funny tonight.

MRS. HAWKINS. I'm not myself. (*laughs lightly*) I guess I'm not myself because of your father's phone call – his taking a later train, like that, for the first time in so many years.

MINNIE. (*with a little giggle*) I don't know what the five-twenty-five will have done without him.

MRS. HAWKINS. (*not sharply*) And all those hoodlums he plays cards with every afternoon.

MINNIE. And all the jokes they make.

(**MRS. HAWKINS** *has been looking straight before her through a window – over the audience's heads, intently.*)

MRS. HAWKINS. There's Mrs. Cochran cooking her dinner.

(*They both gaze absorbedly at Mrs. Cochran a moment.*)

Well, I'm not going to start dinner until your father puts foot in this house.

MINNIE. *(still gazing through the window; slowly)* There's Mr. Cochran at the door...They're arguing about something.

MRS. HAWKINS. Well, that shows that he got in on the five-twenty-five, all right.

MINNIE. Don't people look foolish when you see them, like that – and you can't hear what they're saying? Like ants or something. Somehow, you feel it's not right to look at them when they don't know it.

(They return to their work.)

MRS. HAWKINS. Yes, those men on the train will have missed those awful jokes your father makes.

(MINNIE giggles.)

I declare, Minnie, every year your father makes worse jokes. It's growing on him.

MINNIE. I don't think they're awful, but, I don't understand all of them. Do you? Like what he said to the minister Sunday. I was so embarrassed I didn't want to tell you.

MRS. HAWKINS. I don't want to hear it – not tonight. *(Her gaze returns to the window.)* I can't understand why Mrs. Cochran is acting so strangely. And Mr. Cochran has been coming in and out of the kitchen.

MINNIE. And they seem to keep looking at us all the time.

(After a moment's gazing, they return to their work.)

MRS. HAWKINS. Well, you might as well tell me what your father said to the minister.

MINNIE. I...I don't want to tell you, if it makes you nervous.

MRS. HAWKINS. I've lived with his jokes for twenty years. I guess I can stand one more.

MINNIE. Mr. Brown had preached a sermon about the atom bomb...and about how terrible it would be...and at the church door Papa said to him: "Fine sermon, Joe. I enjoyed it. But have you ever thought of this, Joe" he said – "suppose the atom bomb didn't fall, what would we do then? Have you ever thought of that?" Mr. Brown looked terribly put out.

MRS. HAWKINS. *(puts down her sewing)* He said that!! I declare, he's getting worse. I don't know where he gets such ideas. People will be beginning to think he's bitter. Your father isn't bitter. I know he's not bitter.

MINNIE. No, Mama. People like it. People stop me on the street and tell me what a wonderful sense of humor he has. Like...like... *(she gives up the attempt and says merely)* Oh, nothing.

MRS. HAWKINS. Go on. Say what you were going to say.

MINNIE. What did he mean by saying: "There we sit for twenty years playing cards on the five-twenty-five, hoping that something big and terrible and wonderful will happen – like a wreck, for instance?"

MRS. HAWKINS. *(more distress than indignation)* I say to you seriously, Minnie, it's just self-indulgence. We do everything we know how to make him happy. He loves his home, you know he does. He likes his work – he's proud of what he does at the office. *(She rises and looks down the street through the window at the back. Moved.)* Oh, it's not us he's impatient at: it's the whole world. He simply wishes the whole world were different – that's the trouble with him.

MINNIE. Why, Mama, Papa doesn't complain about anything.

MRS. HAWKINS. Well, I wish he would complain once in a while. *(She returns to her chair.)* For Sunday I'll see if I can't get an extra good bit of veal.

(They sit in silence a moment. The telephone rings.)

Answer that, will you, dear? – No, I'll answer it.

*(***MINNIE*** returns to her work.* ***MRS. HAWKINS*** *has a special voice for answering the telephone, slow and measured.)*

This is Mrs. Hawkins speaking. Oh, yes, Mr. Cochran. What's that? I don't hear you. *(a shade of anxiety)* Are you sure? You must be mistaken.

MINNIE. Mama, what is it?

(MRS. HAWKINS *listens in silence.*)

MINNIE. Mama! Mama!! – What's he saying? Is it about Papa?

MRS. HAWKINS. Will you hold the line one minute, Mr. Cochran? I wish to speak to my daughter. (*She puts her hand over the mouthpiece.*) No, Minnie. It's not about your father at all.

MINNIE. (*rising*) Then what is it?

MRS. HAWKINS. (*in a low, distinct and firm voice*) Now you do what I tell you. Sit down and go on knitting. Don't look up at me and don't show any surprise.

MINNIE. (*a groan of protest*) Mama!

MRS. HAWKINS. There's nothing to be alarmed about – but I want you to obey me. (*She speaks into the telephone.*) Yes, Mr. Cochran...No...Mr. Hawkins telephoned that he was taking a later train tonight. I'm expecting him on the six-thirty. You do what you think best. I'm not sure that's necessary but...you do what you think best. We'll be right here.

(*She hangs up and stands thinking a moment.*)

MINNIE. Mama, I'm almost sixteen. Tell me what it's about.

MRS. HAWKINS. (*returns to her chair; bending over her work, she speaks as guardedly as possible*) Minnie, there's probably nothing to be alarmed about. Don't show any surprise at what I'm about to say to you. Mr. Cochran says that there's been somebody out on the lawn watching us – for ten minutes or more. A man. He's been standing in the shadow of the garage, just looking at us.

MINNIE. (*lowered head*) Is that all!

MRS. HAWKINS. Well, Mr. Cochran doesn't like it. He's...he says he's going to telephone the police.

MINNIE. The police!!

MRS. HAWKINS. Your father'll be home any minute, anyway. (*slight pause*) I guess it's just some...some moody person on an evening walk. Maybe Mr. Cochran's done right to call the police, though. He says that we shouldn't pull the curtains or anything like that – but just act as though nothing has happened. – Now, I don't want you to get frightened.

MINNIE. I'm not, Mama. I'm just...interested. Most nights nothing happens.

MRS. HAWKINS. *(sharply)* I should hope not!

(slight pause)

MINNIE. Mama, all evening I did have the feeling that I was being watched...and that man was being watched by Mrs. Cochran; and *(slight giggle)* Mrs. Cochran was being watched by us.

MRS. HAWKINS. We'll know what it's all about in a few minutes.

(silence)

MINNIE. But Mama, what would the man be looking at? – Just us two sewing.

MRS. HAWKINS. I think you'd better go in the kitchen. Go slowly – and don't look out the window.

MINNIE. *(without raising her head)* No! I'm going to stay right here. But I'd like to know why a man would do that – would just stand and look. Is he...a crazy man?

MRS. HAWKINS. No, I don't think so.

MINNIE. Well, say something about him.

MRS. HAWKINS. Minnie, the world is full of people who think that everybody's happy except themselves. They think their lives should be more exciting.

MINNIE. Does that man think that our lives are exciting, Mama?

MRS. HAWKINS. Our lives are just as exciting as they ought to be, Minnie.

MINNIE. *(with a little giggle)* Well, they are tonight.

MRS. HAWKINS. They are all the time; and don't you forget it.

(The front door bell rings.)

Now, who can that be at the front door? I'll go, Minnie. *(weighing the dangers)* No, you go. – No, I'll go.

(She goes into the hall. The jovial voice of **MR. FORBES** *is heard.)*

MR. FORBES'S VOICE. Good evening, Mrs. Hawkins. Is Herb home?

MRS. HAWKINS'S VOICE. No, he hasn't come home yet, Mr. Forbes. He telephoned that he'd take a later train.

(Enter **MR. FORBES,** *followed by* **MRS. HAWKINS.)**

MR. FORBES. Yes, I know. The old five-twenty-five wasn't the same without him. Darn near went off the rails. *(to* **MINNIE***)* Good evening, young lady.

MINNIE. *(head bent; tiny voice)* Good evening, Mr. Forbes.

MR. FORBES. Well, I thought I'd drop in and see Herb for a minute. About how maybe he'd be wanting a new car – now that he's come into all that money.

MRS. HAWKINS. Come into what money, Mr. Forbes?

MR. FORBES. Why, sure, he telephoned you about it?

MRS. HAWKINS. He didn't say anything about any money.

MR. FORBES. *(laughing loudly)* Well, maybe I've gone and put my foot in it again. So he didn't tell you anything about it yet? Haw-haw-haw. *(confidentially)* If he's got to pay taxes on it we figgered out he'd get about eighteen thousand dollars. – Well, you tell him I called, and tell him that I'll give him nine hundred dollars on that Chevrolet of his – maybe a little more after I've had a look at it.

MRS. HAWKINS. I'll tell him. – Mr. Forbes, I'm sorry I can't ask you to sit down, but my daughter's had a cold for days now and I wouldn't want you to take it home to your girls.

MR. FORBES. I'm sorry to hear that. – Well, as you say, I'd better not carry it with me. *(he goes to the door, then turns and says confidentially)* Do you know what Herb said when he heard that he'd got that money? Haw-haw-haw. I've always said Herb Hawkins has more sense of humor than anybody I know. Why, he said, "All window glass is the same." Haw-haw. "All window glass is the same." Herb! You can't beat him.

MRS. HAWKINS. "All window glass is the same." What did he mean by that?

MR. FORBES. You know: that thing he's always saying. About life. He said it at Rotary in his speech. You know how crazy people look when you see them through a window – arguing and carrying on – and you can't hear a word they say? He says that's the way things look to him. Wars and politics…and everything in life.

(**MRS. HAWKINS** *is silent and unamused.*)

Well, I'd better be going. Tell Herb there's real good glass – unbreakable – on the car I'm going to sell him. Good night, miss; good night, Mrs. Hawkins.

(*He goes out.* **MRS. HAWKINS** *does not accompany him to the front door. She stands a moment looking before her. Then she says, from deep thought.*)

MRS. HAWKINS. That's your father who's been standing out by the garage.

MINNIE. Why would he do that?

MRS. HAWKINS. Looking in. – I should have known it.

MINNIE. (*amazed but not alarmed*) Look! All over the lawn!

MRS. HAWKINS. The police have come. Those are their flashlights.

MINNIE. All over the place! I can hear them talking… (*pause*) …Papa's angry…Papa's very angry. (*They listen.*) Now they're driving away.

MRS. HAWKINS. I should have known it. (*She returns to her seat. Sound of the front door opening and closing noisily.*) That's your father. Don't mention anything unless he mentions it first.

(*They bend over their work. From the hall sounds of* **HAWKINS** *singing the first phrase of "Valencia." Enter* **HAWKINS**, *a commuter. His manner is of loud, forced geniality.*)

HAWKINS. Well – HOW are the ladies?

(*He kisses each lightly on the cheek.*)

MRS. HAWKINS. I didn't start getting dinner until I knew when you'd get here.

HAWKINS. *(largely)* Well, don't start it. I'm taking you two ladies out to dinner. – There's no hurry, though. We'll go to Michaelson's after the crowd's thinned out. *(starting for the hall on his way to the kitchen)* Want a drink, anybody?

MRS. HAWKINS. No. The ice is ready for you on the shelf.

(He goes out. From the kitchen he can be heard singing "Valencia." He returns, glass in hand.)

What kept you, Herbert?

HAWKINS. Nothing. Nothing. I decided to take another train. *(He walks back and forth, holding his glass at the level of his face.)* I decided to take another train. *(He leans teasingly a moment over his wife's shoulder, conspiratorially.)* I thought maybe things might look different through the windows of another train. You know – all those towns I've never been in? Kenniston – Laidlaw – East Laidlaw – Bennsville. Let's go to Bennsville some day. Damn it, I don't know why people should go to Paris and Rome and Cairo when they could go to Bennsville. Bennsville! Oh, Bennsville –

MRS. HAWKINS. Have you been drinking, Herbert?

HAWKINS. This is the first swallow I've had since last night. Oh, Bennsville…breathes there a man with soul so dead –

(MINNIE's eyes have followed her father as he walks about with smiling appreciation.)

MINNIE. I know a girl who lives in Bennsville.

HAWKINS. They're happy there, aren't they? No, not exactly happy, but they live it up to the full. In Bennsville they kick the hell out of life.

MINNIE. Her name's Eloise Brinton.

HAWKINS. Well, Bennsville and East Laidlaw don't look different through the windows of another train. It's not by looking through a train window that you can get at the heart of Bennsville. *(pause)* There all we fellows sit every night on the five-twenty-five playing cards and hoping against hope that there'll be that wonderful, beautiful –

MINNIE. *(laughing delightedly)* Wreck!!

MRS. HAWKINS. Herbert! I won't have you talking that way!

HAWKINS. A wreck, so that we can crawl out of the smoking, burning cars...and get into one of those houses. Do you know what you see from the windows of the train? Those people – those cars – that you see on the streets of Bennsville – they're just dummies. Cardboard. They've been put up there to deceive you. What really goes on in Bennsville – inside those houses – that's what's interesting. People with six arms and legs. People that can talk like Shakespeare. Children, Minnie, that can beat Einstein. Fabulous things.

MINNIE. Papa, I don't mind, but you make Mama nervous when you talk like that.

HAWKINS. Behind those walls. But it isn't only behind those walls that strange things go on. Right on that train, right in those cars. The damndest things. Fred Cochran and Phil Forbes –

MRS. HAWKINS. Mr. Forbes was here to see you.

HAWKINS. Fred Cochran and Phil Forbes – we've played cards together for twenty years. We're so expert at hiding things from one another – we're so cram-filled with things we can't say to one another that only a wreck could crack us open.

MINNIE. *(indicating her mother, reproachfully)* Papa!

MRS. HAWKINS. Herbert Hawkins, why did you stand out in the dark there, looking at us through the window?

HAWKINS. Well, I'll tell you...I got a lot of money today. But more than that I got a message. A message from beyond the grave. From the dead. There was this old lady – I used to do her income tax for her – old lady. She'd keep me on a while – God, how she wanted someone to talk to...I'd say anything that came into my head...I want another drink.

(He goes into the kitchen. Again we hear him singing "Valencia.")

MINNIE. *(whispering)* Eighteen thousand dollars!

MRS. HAWKINS. We've just got to let him talk himself out.

MINNIE. But Mama, why did he go and stand out on the lawn?

MRS. HAWKINS. Shh!

(HAWKINS returns.)

HAWKINS. I told her a lot of things. I told her –

MINNIE. I know! You told her that everything looked as though it were seen through glass.

HAWKINS. Yes, I did. *(pause)* You don't hear the words, or if you hear the words, they don't fit what you see. And one day she said to me: "Mr. Hawkins, you say that all the time: why don't you do it?" "Do what?" I said. "Really stand outside and look through some windows." *(pause)* I knew she meant my own…Well, to tell the truth, I was afraid to. I preferred to talk about it. *(He paces back and forth.)* She died. Today some lawyer called me up and said she's left me twenty thousand dollars.

MRS. HAWKINS. Herbert!

HAWKINS. *(his eyes on the distance)* "To Herbert Hawkins, in gratitude for many thoughtfulnesses and in appreciation of his sense of humor." From beyond the grave… It was an order. I took the four o'clock home…It took me a whole hour to get up the courage to go and stand *(he points)* out there.

MINNIE. But Papa, you didn't see anything! Just us sewing!

(HAWKINS stares before him, then, changing his mood, says briskly.)

HAWKINS. What are we going to have for Sunday dinner?

MINNIE. I know!

HAWKINS. *(pinching her ear)* Buffalo steak?

MINNIE. No.

HAWKINS. I had to live for a week once on rattlesnake stew.

MINNIE. Papa, you're awful.

MRS. HAWKINS. *(putting down her sewing; in an even voice)* Were you planning to go away, Herbert?

HAWKINS. What?

MRS. HAWKINS. *(for the first time, looking at him)* You were thinking of going away.

HAWKINS. *(looks into his glass a moment)* Far away. *(then again putting his face over her shoulder teasingly, but in a serious voice)* There is no "away."…There's only "here." – Get your hats; we're going out to dinner. – I've decided to move to "here." To take up residence, as they say. I'll move in tonight. I don't bring much baggage. – Get your hats.

MRS. HAWKINS. *(rising)* Herbert, we don't wear hats any more. That was in your mother's time. – Minnie, run upstairs and get my blue shawl.

HAWKINS. I'll go and get one more drop out in the kitchen.

MRS. HAWKINS. Herbert, I don't like your old lady.

HAWKINS. *(turning at the door in surprise)* Why, what's the matter with her?

MRS. HAWKINS. I can understand that she was in need of someone to talk to. – What business had she trying to make you look at Minnie and me through windows? As though we were strangers. *(She crosses and puts her sewing on the telephone table.)* People who've known one another as long as you and I have are not supposed to see one another. The pictures we have of one another are inside. – Herbert, last year one day I went to the city to have lunch with your sister. And as I was walking along the street, who do you think I saw coming toward me? From quite a ways off? You! My heart stopped beating and I prayed – I prayed that you wouldn't see me. And you passed by without seeing me. I didn't want you to see me in those silly clothes we wear when we go to the city – and in that silly hat with that silly look we put on our face when we're in public places. The person that other people see.

HAWKINS. *(with lowered eyes)* You saw me – with that silly look.

MRS. HAWKINS. Oh, no. I didn't look long enough for that. I was too busy hiding myself. – I don't know why Minnie's so long trying to find my shawl.

(She goes out. The telephone rings.)

HAWKINS. Yes, this is Herbert Hawkins. – Nat Fischer? Oh, hello, Nat…Oh!…All right. Sure, I see your point of view…Eleven o'clock. Yes, I'll be there. Eleven o'clock.

(He hangs up. **MRS. HAWKINS** *returns wearing a shawl.)*

MRS. HAWKINS. Was that call for me?

HAWKINS. No. It was for me all right. – I might as well tell you now what it was about.

(He stares at the floor.)

MRS. HAWKINS. Well?

HAWKINS. A few minutes ago the police tried to arrest me for standing on my own lawn. Well, I got them over that. But they found a revolver on me – without a license. So I've got to show up at court tomorrow, eleven o'clock.

MRS. HAWKINS. *(short pause; thoughtfully)* Oh…a revolver.

HAWKINS. *(looking at the floor)* Yes…I thought that maybe it was best…that I go away…a long way.

MRS. HAWKINS. *(looking up with the beginning of a smile)* To Bennsville?

HAWKINS. Yes.

MRS. HAWKINS. Where life's so exciting. *(suddenly briskly)* Well, you get the license for that revolver, Herbert, so that you can prevent people looking in at us through the window, when they have no business to. – Turn out the lights when you come.

End of Play

THORNTON WILDER (1897-1975) was an accomplished novelist and playwright whose works explore the connection between the commonplace and the cosmic dimensions of human experience. He won three Pulitzer Prizes: for his novel *The Bridge of San Luis Rey*, and two plays, *Our Town* and *The Skin of Our Teeth*. Wilder's farce, *The Matchmaker*, was adapted as the musical *Hello, Dolly!* He also enjoyed enormous success as a translator, adaptor, actor, librettist and lecturer/teacher. Wilder's many honors include the Gold Medal for Fiction from the American Academy of Arts and Letters and the Presidential Medal of Freedom. Penelope Niven's definitive biography, *Thornton Wilder: A Life*, was published in October 2012. For more information, please visit www.thorntonwilder.com.

Also by
Thornton Wilder...

The Alcestiad

The Beaux' Stratagem (with Ken Ludwig)

The Matchmaker

Our Town

The Skin of Our Teeth

<u>Thornton Wilder One Act Series: The Ages of Man</u>

Infancy

Childhood

Youth

The Rivers Under the Earth

<u>Thornton Wilder One Act Series: Wilder's Classic One Acts</u>

The Long Christmas Dinner

Queens of France

Pullman Car Hiawatha

Love and How to Cure It

Such Things Only Happen in Books

The Happy Journey to Trenton and Camden

<u>Thornton Wilder One Act Series: The Seven Deadly Sins</u>

The Drunken Sisters

Bernice

The Wreck on the 5:25

A Ringing of Doorbells

In Shakespeare and the Bible

Someone From Assisi

Cement Hands

Please visit our website **samuelfrench.com** for complete descriptions and licensing information.

www.ingramcontent.com/pod-product-compliance
Lightning Source LLC
Chambersburg PA
CBHW071848290426
44109CB00017B/1966